Marine Mammals

WALRUSES

ZELDA KING

PowerKiDS
press™

New York

Published in 2012 by The Rosen Publishing Group, Inc.
29 East 21st Street, New York, NY 10010

First Edition

Editor: Joanne Randolph
Book Design: Julio Gil

Photo Credits: Cover Joseph Van Os/The Image Bank/Getty Images; pp. 4, 5, 7, 8 (top), 9, 11, 12–13, 16 Shutterstock.com; pp. 6, 20–21 Norbert Rosing/National Geographic/Getty Images; pp. 8 (bottom), 11 iStockphoto/Thinkstock; pp. 10, 15 Jupiterimages/Photos.com/Thinkstock; p. 14 (top) Ralph Lee Hopkins/National Geographic/Getty Images; p. 14 (bottom) © www.iStockphoto.com/Tersina Shieh; p. 17 Paul Souders/Stone/Getty Images; p. 18 © www.iStockphoto.com/Evgeniya Lazareva; p. 19 © www.iStockphoto.com/Erlend Kvalsvik; p. 22 Paul Nicklen/National Geographic/Getty Images.

Library of Congress Cataloging-in-Publication Data

King, Zelda.
 Walruses / by Zelda King. — 1st ed.
     p. cm. — (Marine mammals)
 Includes index.
 ISBN 978-1-4488-5005-1 (library binding) — ISBN 978-1-4488-5141-6 (pbk.) — ISBN 978-1-4488-5142-3 (6-pack)
 1. Walrus—Juvenile literature. I. Title. II. Series.
 QL737.P62K56 2012
 599.79'9—dc22

                               2010048086

Manufactured in the United States of America

CPSIA Compliance Information: Batch #WS11PK: For Further Information contact Rosen Publishing, New York, New York at 1-800-237-9932

CONTENTS

Wonderful Walruses

Have you ever seen a walrus? These **marine mammals** are famous for their huge bodies, wrinkled skin, **whiskers**, and long **tusks**. Walruses are social animals that form strong friendships with other walruses. They will hurry to help another walrus in trouble.

Do you know where the word "walrus" comes from? It comes from the Old Norse word *hvalros*, which means "sea horse" or "sea cow." Scientists call the walrus *Odobenus*

Walruses come on land in large groups, called colonies. Young walruses are brown, while older walruses are reddish brown.

rosmarus. Odobenus is a Greek word meaning "tooth walker." Walruses got that name because they pull themselves out of the water with their long tusks.

Walruses' tusks can be around 3 feet (1 m) long. Males have longer and thicker tusks than females do.

What Type of Walrus Is It?

There are two main types of walruses. They are Atlantic walruses and Pacific walruses. They get their names from the oceans in which they live.

There are about 22,500 Atlantic walruses. Males, or bulls, weigh about 2,000 pounds (907 kg) and are about 8 feet (2 m) long. Females, or cows, are a little smaller.

There are about 10 times more Pacific walruses than Atlantic walruses. They are darker than Atlantic walruses and can be

Atlantic walruses generally have smaller tusks and are smaller in size than Pacific walruses.

much larger. Males can weigh up to about 3,750 pounds (1,700 kg) and be 12 feet (4 m) long. That is the size of a car! Just as with Atlantic walruses, female Pacific walruses are smaller.

These Pacific walruses have climbed out of the water to rest on a rocky shore.

Where in the World Are Walruses?

You already know that walruses live in the Atlantic Ocean and the Pacific Ocean. However, they do not live everywhere in those oceans. They live only in the far northern parts, in the icy cold **Arctic** waters. Pacific walruses, which number more than 200,000, live around Alaska and northern Russia.

Both kinds of walruses like to live in the icy waters of the Arctic. To keep them warm in these cold places, they have thick skin and up to 6 inches (15 cm) of blubber underneath it.

Where Walruses Live

Asia

Arctic Region

North America

MAP KEY

- Pacific Walrus
- Atlantic Walrus

The 22,500 Atlantic walruses live around northeastern Canada and Greenland.

Walruses do not live in the deep ocean. They live along shores and near **pack ice**. The land and ice give them places where they can come out of the water to rest and lie in the sun.

9

Whiskers, Flippers, and a Body of Blubber

If you lived where walruses do, how would you stay warm? Walruses have heavy coats, though it is not their fur that keeps them warm. Under their skin, they have **blubber** that is up to 6 inches (15 cm) thick!

Like other pinnipeds, walruses have **flippers**. They swim with their back flippers. Their front flippers control their direction.

A walrus's upper lip can have up to 700 whiskers. These whiskers are special. They are almost like

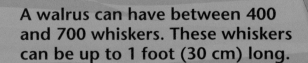

A walrus can have between 400 and 700 whiskers. These whiskers can be up to 1 foot (30 cm) long.

fingers. They are very good at feeling. Walruses use them to find food on the ocean floor, where it is hard to see. The whiskers also help carry food into a walrus's mouth!

Did You Know?

Arctic waters are so cold that ice is always present. Even the highest temperature is below freezing. In July, the water is only 29° F (-2° C)!

Walrus's flippers have the same bones as arms and hands but they have changed over time to help the walrus swim in water.

My, What Long Tusks You Have!

What do walruses have that other pinnipeds do not? Tusks! The tusks of the bull can reach 39 inches (1 m) and weigh 12 pounds (5 kg)! The cow has smaller tusks. They grow to be about 30 inches (76 cm) long.

Why do walruses need these huge tusks? They serve many purposes. They break breathing holes in ice. They help walruses pull themselves out of the water onto ice or land, too. Bulls show their tusks to tell other bulls how powerful they are. Bulls also use their tusks to fight other bulls and enemies.

Did You Know?

A walrus's teeth can tell us how old the animal was when it died. If you cut crosswise through a walrus tooth, you will see rings. Each ring equals one year that that walrus lived.

This male walrus is showing off its long tusks. Walruses can have between 18 and 38 other teeth in their mouths.

Huge, Noisy Herds

Like people, walruses are social animals. They form herds because they enjoy being together. Bulls and cows form separate herds. These herds are huge. Hundreds or even thousands of animals may gather together! Walruses also like to touch each other. They crowd together and pile on top of one another.

Above: Walruses are known for being noisy. *Right*: They are also known for fighting. Males fight over space and over their group of females during mating season.

Males and females generally form separate herds but come together to mate. Females also form nursery herds with their young.

Walruses talk to each other using many different sounds. They make growls, barks, tapping sounds, whistles, and clicks. Imagine how noisy a huge herd must be! When it is time to **mate**, bulls sing long songs to get the attention of cows.

What Walruses Eat

Although walruses are huge, they eat mostly small animals from the ocean floor. Clams are their favorite food. Walruses also eat other **mollusks** and soft animals like snails, worms, and octopuses. Sometimes, they eat fish and small seals.

As you can imagine, it takes a lot of small animals to feed a walrus. An adult walrus can eat 5,000 clams at one time!

The ocean floor is dark. Walruses feel for food

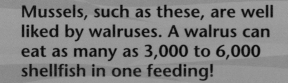

Mussels, such as these, are well liked by walruses. A walrus can eat as many as 3,000 to 6,000 shellfish in one feeding!

with their whiskers and lips. When they find mollusks, they suck the animals out of their shells. Walruses do not chew their food. They swallow it whole!

Walruses use their upper lips to dig for food on the seafloor. They may shoot jets of water at the seafloor to get at animals under the sand, too.

Arctic Enemies

Walruses have few natural enemies because of their size. After all, there are not many animals that can kill **prey** the size of a car! Few animals can bite through the walrus's thick skin either.

Polar bears eat walrus calves. They catch the calves by scaring a walrus herd on land and causing cows and calves to become separated. Sometimes, polar bears attack small groups of walruses on ice sheets floating on the water.

Orcas are fierce hunters that swim in the same waters where walruses live.

Killer whales, or orcas, attack walruses in the water. Like polar bears, the whales mostly go after calves. They may also attack adults that have been hurt, though.

Polar bears are known to charge walrus herds. They then eat any animals that were hurt as the walruses rushed to escape.

19

The Life of a Walrus

You likely weighed less than 10 pounds (4.5 kg) when you were born. A newborn walrus weighs 100 pounds (45 kg) or more! It has soft gray or brown fur and whiskers but no tusks. It can swim right away. Cows feed their calves rich milk to help them grow quickly. They also teach them how to find food, keep them safe, and play with them.

After two or three years, calves leave their mothers. Young cows stay with their herds. Young bulls join bull herds. In a few years, the youngsters become adults and have their own calves. Walruses can live to be 40 years old.

Here an Atlantic walrus and her calf rest on the pack ice. Walrus females generally have only one baby at a time. They have new babies every two or more years.

A World Without Walruses?

Walruses have long lives and few natural enemies. You might think there will always be walruses. However, they do have one deadly enemy. People are the biggest danger these animals face.

For thousands of years, people have hunted walruses for their meat, skin, blubber, and tusks. By the 1800s, walruses had almost disappeared. Today, laws allow only native people of the Arctic to hunt them. However, **poachers** kill them for their prized tusks.

People have done other things that put walruses in danger, too. Ocean **pollution** harms them. **Global warming** melts the pack ice they need. If people do not take care of these wonderful animals, the world may one day be without walruses.

Native people, such as the Inuits, are the only people who can lawfully hunt walruses. They count on the walrus for food.

GLOSSARY

Arctic (ARK-tik) The land and water near the North Pole.

blubber (BLUH-ber) The fat of a whale, penguin, walrus, or other sea animal.

flippers (FLIH-perz) Broad, flat body parts suited for swimming.

global warming (GLOH-bul WAWRM-ing) A gradual increase in how hot Earth is. It is caused by gases that are released when people burn fuels such as gasoline.

mammals (MA-mulz) Warm-blooded animals that have backbones and hair, breathe air, and feed milk to their young.

marine (muh-REEN) Having to do with the sea.

mate (MAYT) To come together to make babies.

mollusks (MAH-lusks) Animals without backbones and with soft bodies and, often, shells.

pack ice (PAK EYS) A mass of sea ice formed by the pushing together of ice floes and other pieces of ice.

poachers (POH-cherz) People who illegally kill animals that are protected by the law.

pollution (puh-LOO-shun) Man-made waste that harms Earth's air, land, or water.

prey (PRAY) An animal that is hunted by another animal for food.

tusks (TUSKS) Long, large pointed teeth that come out of the mouths of some animals.

whiskers (HWIS-kerz) Long, thin, hard hairs on an animal's face.

INDEX

WEB SITES

Due to the changing nature of Internet links, PowerKids Press has developed an online list of Web sites related to the subject of this book. This site is updated regularly. Please use this link to access the list:

www.powerkidslinks.com/marm/walrus/